TEACH ME, DEAR SISTER

ALSO BY IRVING FELDMAN

Works and Days
The Pripet Marshes
Magic Papers
Lost Originals
Leaping Clear
New and Selected Poems

TEACH ME, DEAR SISTER

poems by

IRVING FELDMAN

The Viking Press / New York
Penguin Books

Penguin Books Ltd, Harmondsworth,
Middlesex, England
Penguin Books, 40 West 23rd Street,
New York, New York 10010, U.S.A.
Penguin Books Australia Ltd, Ringwood,
Victoria, Australia
Penguin Books Canada Limited, 2801 John Street,
Markham, Ontario, Canada L3R 1B4
Penguin Books (N.Z.) Ltd, 182–190 Wairau Road,
Auckland 10, New Zealand

First published in 1983 in simultaneous hardcover and paperback editions
by The Viking Press and Penguin Books, 40 West 23rd Street, New York,
New York 10010
Published simultaneously in Canada
Copyright © 1980, 1981, 1982, 1983 by Irving Feldman
All rights reserved

LIBRARY OF CONGRESS CATALOGING IN PUBLICATION DATA
Feldman, Irving, 1928–
Teach me, dear sister.
I. Title.
PS3511.E23T4   1983   811'.54   82-70131
ISBN 0-670-31135-9 (hardcover)
ISBN 0 14 042.302 8 (paperback)

I wish to thank the New York State Council on the Arts and the Ingram
Merrik Foundation, whose grants enabled me to complete this volume.—I.F.

"The Bathers," "Fresh Air" (originally titled "Social Constructions of Reality
at Coney Island"), "Just Another Smack," and "Progress" were originally
published in *Poetry* magazine.

Other poems were previously published in *Antaeus, Grand Street, Greenfield
Review, The Kenyon Review, The Nation, The New Republic, Shenandoah, Vir-
ginia Quarterly Review,* and *Yale Review*; an excerpt from an interview by Tad
Prozewicz with Philip Levine appeared in *Antaeus* in Summer 1980.

Printed in the United States of America
Set in Caslon

To Willie Feldman,
my father

CONTENTS

TEACH ME, DEAR SISTER

MILLIONS OF
STRANGE SHADOWS

Courtesy came before joy,
the greeting preceded the recognition.
I thought it would pass me by, the great crowd
that came singing itself home from the feast
(where I was heading—too late! I thought),
and raised my arm as passersby do
in the street, nodding vaguely as if to say,
Yes, that *is* you—whoever you are.
(And thought, But they left the party too soon.)

Whoever they were: all those forgotten,
those still to arrive, faceless, familiar,
singing, and flowing after their song,
millions of strange shadows, strange lights,
that rose from darkness, that now came close,
gleamed in salutation, spoke my name.
The voices made it new and the same,
not mine only—theirs to call me by.
And though I alone was flesh there,
shadow and light and song pressed around,
escorted me wholly among them
—they the true body in which I walked,
the words that made my throat veridical,
and here the feast that roamed the roads
and sang in the streets from dawn to dawn.

THE BATHERS

Can there be women alone and no serpent near?

The haze conceals a hint, the hint a presence . . .

Student of opportunities, he licks the air . . .
"Who are these, flittering swift perfumes,
this pair of pairs,
in two-piece swimsuits,
two black, two blood-red,
in taut and ruffled satin,
waves of their hair waves of the sea?"

Touch one anywhere and you are touched by all
—so every raindrop holds the whole sea.

"Who are these strangers,
with sharp little teeth and little pink tongues,
deftly clicking bobby pins apart
or running a thumb along a halter strap
—strangers but as if intended?"

He moves by mere percipience,
his senses draw near.

"Who lifts an arm, who shakes her curls,
flirting with the universe

—just to show the others she *can*,
just to let it know who's there?"

Sways elaborate kinks aloft,
preens his keen head.
"But who are they, after all?"

Oiling their arms and fiddling with their hair,
making it behave, not be such a bother,
sprawled or sitting one to a blanket corner,
all combed alike, all made up alike, all
dressed in the uniform of loveliness,
and each the queen of her brilliant parlor,
what can North Star be telling South Wind,
blond Sunrise express to West's brunette
with eyebrows arching, with shrugging shoulder?
"I love cerise!" "I can't stand chartreuse!"
"Me, I'm just crazy about egg-clairs!"
"Kessler's napoleons . . . they're much too sweet!"
"My sister's new jumper is really cute!"
—precious tastes by which they mean to say
that not all raindrops are the same,
as if they could make themselves crystalline,
as if they were not constantly flowing away,
waves of their hair waves of the sea . . .

The beach's whole ear, he would listen forever . . .

Too innocent to sense the serpent there?
that certain air of consciousness
in the air? Not letting on,

excited, they talk louder—to civilize
the creature, to tame the bold fella, whisper
to coax him closer . . . teach him this
is how you treat a girl, this is what
a lady likes, this is how he must say,
how run her errands like any common
kid brother (no harm if he thinks himself
her pet), how stand there charming not
scary, now lay his head harmless halfway up
on her milky thigh . . . till devil himself
would hold still to have his toenails painted
and beg favor to rest on her the sunlamp
of his exclusive attending, be her own,
her private particular sun . . . so great
her neediness is, so great must be
his services—his servitude for her distress,
drowning in beingness—as constant
and changing, as endless as the sea . . .

"The wind's coquetting hem,
wave's dark underneath and white release
—brightness too brief!"
His single name for the glittering
of opportunity is woman.

Every girl has a dream, every woman a story.

If she makes excuse, saying, *"It'll mess my hair!"*
"It's too cold today!" *"Really, I'm still full!"*
"Oh, I just finished putting my lotion on!"
if she doesn't walk out into the whole

embrace and flowing—then has nothing to say
when she goes among other women
telling their fibs fibs fibs, and must sit there
like a dummy without two cents to chip in.
If she doesn't, the little pitcher
of her lap pours nothing out,
no stain will darken down her skirt
its uncontrollable sap of sorrows and time
while she looks at herself unbelieving
—betrayed betrayed! If she doesn't,
there's no gathering her womb's wet spillage,
and never will learn she has nothing, is
nothing herself, no domain, no house, no land,
servant to everyone's hunger, discarded
afterward, if not devoured during,
her one inheritance her own nerve
—oh *must* have her way, since she has nothing else.
And later, no laying out the dead,
no lamentation, submission, surviving,
no letting the lid down gently,
and letting drop the tiny hidden trump:
denied the first, oh sweetness always of
the last word and taking off the last trick
and leaving the table utterly bare,
and sitting on before the dark waves opening
and closing their jaws over the bare beach
while she says her story out to the sea,
"I *have* been bloody and I *will* be
a bellyache to the wave that takes me!"
—and always pleasure of the whole deck
snug and full in the palm of her hand

while everything else goes on and on
being nothing—unless she lets it be her:
even losses enlarge her, her secrets, lies
—a fate with the fortunes asleep in her fist—
so massive now that nothing escapes,
so great she hardly knows all she is,
but *feels* it whenever waves come
and do pretty please to her feet . . .

Day toward evening; discreetly,
the serpent recedes, seeming to bow and waving,
takes up a post among the shadows, waiting . . .
Who are these bright flecks carried along
on the tiding flank, still speaking?

"My mother needs me!"
"I promised my sister!"
"My father wants me to help!"
"My boyfriend's waiting!"
To be required, requested, rich
in society, in obligations, not
less or left behind, and belong
wholly to their time, as if they were not
flowing away . . . They pack up, go heavily
—the graces of dawn are donkeys at five
in service to what old discipline of bearing,
opportunity to others but such problems
to themselves, dull silhouettes lumped out
with comforting bundles, bulk and clutter
of being, cards, a shoe dangled, clothing . . .
a little while longer their radio's

portable rumba stays on dancing alone
above the sand it will not stir at this
late hour . . . looses its last little thunder . . .
No animal in sight, north or south, east
or west, no likely chance, no lively wager . . .

A serpent alone and no women near?

Waves have licked the beach clear.

"But who are these,
lightly daring forward,
who approach, who appear?"

THEY

Adam alone had been Adam
unknown, shadowless under
the sun, lost in shadow under
the moon, lost in thought that thought
all things and found their names, and yet
could not find Adam in its thought.

The thought beyond Adam's thinking
grew visible and saw:
Adam abandoned, unwitting.
In her regard he saw himself thought,
in her thought found himself, found
Adam. His lips parted. Adam.

Endeared to himself in a globe
of thought, now Adam thought
multitudes of Adam
vanishing toward purity
—himself, a column, line, a point,
then volumes of inanition.

Pity him! the serpent whispered,
placing the knowledge on her palm.
It was round and simple and shining:
You see how he consumes himself,
he is dying. She saw,

and offered the fruit, meaning:
of her might Adam eat
without himself falling to food
—of her, of Eve, he could eat.
Then Adam lay there, sated, sleeping.

Figures crowded his dream in glory
—while she, who desired only
the bright raiment of his gaze, now saw
her nakedness of food, food
he had dared and then possessed, then
surpassed, he, sealed as himself, as
Adam—ungrateful, starving.

What was she to herself in thought?
As little as thought could be to her?
She needed him bitterly
to raise her being to his lips,
cherish her lowliness by eating.
Descend into blindness, into
simplicity? be food again?
his food? less and less Eve?
sweeten herself all over?
despised again? devoured again?

Forgive him! the serpent hissed.

A CRONE'S TALE

to Françoise Krampf

Tell you of the witch? Well, so I will, child,
as well as ever I remember the story.
Now the witch was an ordinary girl
and not half so pretty as you, and like you
grew up to her life on an island's small place.
And seeing there the changeable wilderness
of water, that plashed and sparkled among rocks
and stroked the sand, then fussing and wilful chased
the little boats from their paths, and later
was wide shining distance, indifferent to all
and different from everybody—seeing this,
why then, she set her heart on the mystery.
And so she stood and called out names to the sea,
every name that ever the girl could think.
Now you must take care, child, what names you say.
Your cry for help, your offer of kindness,
both sup together in the name you speak.
So you must take care to what name you answer.
Now I will tell you the ocean heard her.
As foreign sailormen it came ashore,
well, and every day more of them came and more,
strange hollering things that stood up in the foam
like waterfalls, or on hands and knees trickled
to the windy beach and lay about drying,
or came like spraywater by the stinging wind
blown there, beardy and rough and rimed with salt.

Well, as sailormen the sea came ashore,
as animals it stayed on there, listening
to nice syllables spelled clear in her breath,
they the wild element's soft embodiment,
they enchanted slowly to domestic ways.
Now, child, you have seen the salamander, how
it lies in the winter hearth sunning on coals
and laving off ash with licks of its tongue,
and you have heard the air's sprites in the wood,
and seen the grizzled field lift a green head
and dart the dainty tines of its silent tongue.
Just so in her stable were round strange backs
running like waves under the drover wind
and many snouts were leaping up together
and butty heads slapping the whitewash posts,
and rushes in fury and fright, and patience
nibbling along inside the green centuries.
Many were swine there, and never swine only,
but sheep they were, too, both mister and missus,
yes, hens and horses, geese and goats and cattle
—now let me see, who is it I have forgot?—
and whiteface rabbits and many mice as well,
all trampling up the one scatter of straw
and taking molasses, taking stews and slops,
good things to eat she fixed in the kitchen,
green things that in her garden sprouted up.
And came to her running ever she called them,
"You, Henry," "You, Alfred," "You, Charles," and such,
good names all, such names they were as your brothers
would have and kings of the happiest place.
Or came if ever they heard clump of her shoes

or kirtle whisper to the hay's shining raff.
Well she knew it was the sea in her stable
that came to glint there with thousand bright eyes
and pricked up ears and made eager noises, nudged
her hand with moist noses, sucked on her fingers,
that sat down guest at her floor's low table,
that warmed itself in itself in its sleep.
And ever we want, child, the creatures by,
to have the good of them, the milk and mildness,
so must we do with victuals and kind voices.
Oh, if that were enough! But there's more than it.
Here now, I've dropped my thimble, just wait a bit.
Run, sweet, and pick it up where it rolls away
under that chair, I can just see its gleaming.
There, that's the good child . . .
Well, as I was saying, she kept the straw clean,
she freshened the water, she did not scant
the poor sailormen that came to her shore.
But one of them she would by no means feed,
by no means would she call him to her,
but left him to roam the shoreline all day
and wade the white streets of the broken wave.
Him alone she kept a stranger, until
the night long when beasts snugged down in their sleep
he only cried out "Circe, Circe" to her
as if the sea's self with a human voice
at last would single out, would summon her.
And ever all night she was held around,
but she bit back the word, by no means would speak.
She thought she drowned, and then she didn't drown.
I forget what happens next, but no matter.

Now the girl had what most her heart wanted.
She lived on an island, she married the sea.

It may be you shall think one day to marry.
It may be you shall walk beside the water,
hearing it keen the feeling it cannot say.
Then must you put fingers to ears, lock eyes shut
—or shall in pity cry out names to it,
shall hunt its far shine in every eye comes near.
Or it may be you shall never . . .
Here now lay your finger on this knot. Just so.
And from deeps may come to you a daughter.
Perhaps shall call the child for me . . .

So now your old grandmother, as fond as old,
gives you her blessing, and a kiss goes with it.
Remember her name in your prayer every night.
So out goes candle now—now you must go to sleep.

EBERHEIM

Eberheim, *je pense à vous*
—or try to, though unable
to bring you into any field
of vision: in Vladivostok
buried as another, the narrator
having followed the wrong cortege
one hundred pages after
your first appearance in the novel:*
that "horrible groan" (they waited,
fruitlessly, for a second) from
an "adjoining room"—in Petersburg
where, coincident
to bloody skirmishing in the streets,
you were beginning
to begin your dying.
Your "life" two brief notices
of two phantom events,
and your obituary
three glances meeting to agree
you were better off so.
No showing forth here—even
an epiphany in a brown woolen suit
would have been brighter—rather,
a hiding away, a vanishing.

* *William Gerhardie's* Futility

What *can* resolve your image?
—pity must blur the whole
in bloating the detail,
irony diminish all
for clarity's small sake.
"Elderly," "penniless," "exacting,"
shyest of all the entries in
the who's who in solitude
—how *is* one to place
an exemplary irrelevance?—
half-expunged, fugitive, yet familiar,
like the brother of a famous face,
and even less than ink on paper
—Eberheim, I think of you!

THE BIOGRAPHIES
OF SOLITUDE

Blue the hills, red the fields,
where the kisses and blows were dealt . . .
How eager they were, marching away,
enlistees in the horde of love.
Farewell the sweethearts
—they never came back.
Welcome, sisters of solitude.

And who will say these lives have been?

Solitude has no biographers.

Nonetheless, hands move across the pages.
Nonetheless, empty pages go from hand to hand.
Nonetheless, papers blow over the landscape
of magical names, the beautiful promises.

One is in snowy Idaho, raging.
One in California sits before her mirror,
considering death.
One takes hot baths in Tennessee,
to calm herself, calm herself down.
In Kansas one scribbles madly.
One walks in a daze in the crowds
on Forty-second Street, barefoot,

her feet bruised, day after day.
In the hospital of the wind.

What the flood has spared is given
into the keeping of the whirlwind.

Day after day the wind
numbering the losses . . .

"From now on I will love only myself."
"I no longer try to make sense to people."
"It's all a game anyway."
"Back then I still had my ideals.
No sacrifice was too much for me.
I was strong. I felt everything."
"I don't even pity myself anymore."

They bite their lips.
Shrug their shoulders.

"What is there left to protect?"
"Who can you trust?"

How America is immense and filled with solitudes!

IN OLD SAN JUAN

I've come to visit Doña Trina,
to pay respects and receive my blessing.
At the kitchen table under the great clock
where an elegy is always ticking,
this is me sitting mute in the center of
her amphitheater of darkening photos:
children and their children, nieces, nephews,
while Doña Trina fussing to one side
plays the prompter with sherry and whispers
—So many successes, such lovely spouses.
Can age be the good thief who's carried off
every bitter word she may once have known?
Her small talk levitates a world of praise.
And I must say they are looking down at me
in the kindest way, as sweetly as the cakes
from the icebox, the *turrón* on the table,
or Doña Trina sugaring my ear.
For all the fan's dulcet stirring, it's hot
in here, I feel in danger of becoming
gingerbread in this nice lady's oven
—nothing can be *this* sweet!
                    Ay, Doña Trina,
your tales can't make good so much betrayal.
Who could believe the little show-offs
would go so far, and so far away, become
doctors, lawyers, *professionals*?—oh,

the shamelessness of all epiphanies!
Why do we insist on growing our faces,
when one might instead have been a sunny wall?
Such heartbreaking gleams leap from photographs
of youth's full cheeks or fresh little moustache,
Latin style, circa nineteen-fifty!
Somebody strike me blind before
I glimpse my own opacity
—obese with accomplishment, I obscure
as I impress, abashed when I think,
Who could ever dream over all this flesh?
Set me, Doña Trina, among your pride
of photos on the piano couchant,
or on your mantelpiece to keep the time
with two syllables only,
tick for things, *tock* for nothingness,
and let me hear you murmur, twittering, wise,
not how far I've come but how much I promise.

THE SALON
OF FAMOUS BABIES

Of course, she knew he loved her, but how he did
nagged at her and pestered, refused to shut up.
No, she wouldn't mince the words in her mind:
it seemed just ordinary stupid love,
ignorant, or unaware, of itself, of her,
so unobservant, so lacking in detail
it was almost, *almost* an insult—she
would not have loved a puppy so!

                               Well, here
was something that needed doing, and when
she loved now it wasn't that simple old love,
but serious, *teaching* love, love that would show him
what loving really was, working, taking pains,
thinking things out.

                        It put her in a rage
how little he saw even this, even now!
As well teach ducks to drown as teach him not
to take it all as owed the world's own son and heir.
Oh, *his* idea of love was feeling fine
and saying *Bless you* and *Okay* to everything,
and nodding *Hey* in her direction, where maybe
he sensed some pleasant thickening in the glow.
He thought love was checking in to count the house,
and his daydream of glory always the feature,
with maybe in the gawking crowds her face
repeated a thousand tiny times (at least that,

dear god!) in the last row under the rafters.
She saw it in his eyes sometimes—and it cut
to the quick to see him . . . so, so *limited*,
how in everything he did a little man
inclined lazily in a little bow.

No, no,

no, loving meant alertness, meant knowing her
bit by bit *and* (enthusiasm had added
had not prudence disallowed it) *through and through!*
What saved her patience was pitying him:
that trim, self-sufficient poverty of his,
which never even dreamt what worlds it missed
—a thousand vitalities ablaze each instant
around his head . . . that once a week some thunder struck.
Why, anyone with any wickedness in her
might truss and stuff him, and go her way whistling.
Lucky for him, *she* was no empty shell like those,
she had feeling still, had kept her soul intact
and always would—if only *he* were man enough
to stand up to her and fight back.

Nonetheless,

she felt her powers come: she knew—it had to go
without saying—that she was his superior.
Let him elevate that noble brow of his
in the salon of the famous babies, *she* knew
—just didn't she—*who* was the lion's hairdresser!
Oh, it might have been restful there beside him
—so slow, so unwitting—she'd have napped a bit,
but the injustice kept picking into her heart,
and she muttered *How dare he! How dare he!*
a thousand times, until she thought it once

—the thought transformed her forever—*Why, he dares!*
Amazed, she understood something awful,
that he was careless, dull, unattending from
a vast strength he had in secret: he knew
he couldn't be hurt.

                So, it *is* a man's world,
she thought. Grand and mysterious, the summit
of his self-confidence rose from her very feet.
Everything had been a preparation—this
would be her crowning work: to climb to its top
and look around—oh, she would blink at nothing—
and see whatever was out there to see.
She would take the world's measure and, if it came
to not much, infer the mountain didn't either.
She was prepared for that, prepared to render
objective and final judgment on it all,
and then say if the climb was worth it or not
(on the whole, she'd guess, not), but would decide later
whether to publish her report.

                    In any case
and certainly, she would *not* be defeated.

BEAUTY

Jewish Brooklyn's bit of Muscovite winter,
Christmas Eve of 'forty or 'forty-one,
I and papa struggling in wind and snow
on a dark land's end of empty avenue.
Suddenly she was there—seen once before,
not ever since—staggering from a side street,
superb woman some s.o.b. had knocked around,
punched six steps up from a musty basement flat,
tall, black, battered, regal, coatless, drunk, beautiful.
She caught my breath, catches my breath again
—exiled queen of a scattered warrior people,
or Venus led in chains, who hurls her shivered spear
forty years flying into the afterworld.
Beauty not to be battered down, love defeated.

TO WHAT'S-HER-NAME

Being there together could be too hot
for comfort, but that density of life
in common made us zip and buzz, and sting.
We knew our flutterings mattered—the future
was us impatient to become itself,
and our chatter, all those nasty or tasty
predicates mere excuses to revisit
the loud patch of our intoxicating names.
That rant of pollination fevered more
than anything, than any single passion could!
And now we're thinned out, all gone off to die
or be the scene's newest young hothead's
or hot young thing's dull bumbling ancestor
—and even you are full of irrelevant
reminiscences, as if too deranged
to do more than hover, you whose beauty shows
in all these scarred disreputable gashes.

Back when your gentle attentions were picking
my heart clean in plain sight of everyone,
did I ever dream that, in pity for
your crumpled lips, I'd regret your smile's faint
fume of vitriol, your sudden awful
gulped-down squeal when you inched in for the kill,
the ready shameless hot gush of your gossip,
always virulent, always victorious?

ALBERT FEINSTEIN

1

No angel does this: thickens, goes white.
Then some are born old, perhaps?
Not so the stern juvenile of distance,
Apollo staring from the sun, confirming
or destroying in the light of day,
as if youth itself were a judgment.
But then these old, purblind ones, craning
and pressing close to us?—Whispers,
or less, our lips just beginning
to part, a thought unspoken, hardly owned,
lights in them a pure intelligence.
Nameless or never rightly named,
and yet their faces glow.
                              This one,
for example, hovering beside
two student actors like their guardian
(darkness, an empty theater, the trio there
on stage, whom I, a stranger killing time,
have come across by accident),
—someone's called him "Albert Feinstein."
Albert *Fein*stein? Albert Feinstein
coaching college theatricals?
But Albert was a young man
when I last saw him thirty years ago,
as young as the clod playing "Adam,"

as poor "Eve": pedantic wanting
to be winsome, coming out cute.
We were young poets together!
sleek littermates in the epoch's wallow,
nursed and farted side by side.
His style was drowsy and whimsical,
like one who's unprepared but unsurprised.
Oh I half remembered the elegant stoop
thickened here to tortoise plate,
but not the silver error flagrant on his brow.
Why, he could be my father now!
But look at his face, see—what can
have made the witty fool grow beautiful?

2

So many years some handfuls of sensitive earth,
such artless "Adam"s and silly "Eve"s, who can't
express the sense they have by heart—and yet
their pain of shortcoming is bliss in him.
See, he is looking from one to the other,
radiant and mute and keen, his face lit with
the good intention waylaid in their clay.
See, he sets them in his circle of patience,
this bit of the fullness of time, all the time
in the world in a little sphere—where they play.
It is the least precipitous, the gentlest joy
—patience that overgrows the deadlines instant
by instant, that ripens the intimate minute.
"If not this time, then another time
. . . it is all *one* time," his attending implies.
And they understand it is a joy to repeat,

however poorly, because joy to be here
with one another and with this third
who makes their love possible, *is* their love
made visible to them, a quiet angel
they place in the keeping of happiness.
See, he has been cast into his own life,
in a drama greater than he directs.
Here Adam and Eve say each other's name,
there Feinstein ages into innocence.
See, because of Feinstein we go on trying,
the clod heaves himself up and turns over,
the girl grows solemn and deep, the globe shines.

THE DROWNED MAN

We open our eyes and the world is light,
a radiance that opens our eyes.
As each of us has dreamed it,
so it is now in the sight of all
—cordial and plain and total.
Why waken here if not in greeting
to the embassy of everything?
Dreaming, I knew it would be so, but not
how like my dream, how truly known, how glowing.

A consciousness gone, a radiance lost.
The world is diminished by a world.
The embassy has tarried on the way.
The common light appears, displaced and dazed,
verbless, unresponsive, a stranger
who has closed his eyes—and if he dreams
our sweet breath after swimming and then
our little sleep, will never say; and we,
like the light, enfeebled, cannot wake him or speak.

TEACH ME,
DEAR SISTER

Teacher, muse, sibyl.
Three times in three guises
she appeared to him.

*

Her great eight to his five importunate years,
she sat him and they played at school.
Big steaming pots of sun, their kitchen classroom,
where he, the simplest Simon anywhere,
did this, did that, as she would tell him to.
Then, one morning, he saw the world take form:
outlined in simple rules, and for subtle hue
her sober intoning, her sage and tender frown.
Alert to please, before she could say,
he sat up straighter, he listened carefully,
he told his swinging legs to stop
—bright baby ape who deftly locked the cage
door shut, then proudly handed back the key.
Gladness was: to be his better self,
to make her happy eyes, her brow be smooth.
His body stilled, his mind raced forward.
Everything everywhere could be something known,
and precious suddenly for being knowledge,
though not truly known until made known to her.
Her eyes were dark and kind. To them he sped
the little love bullets of his replies,
tidbits of world he would set before her.

Of all arguing dumbbells everywhere,
he alone rang out true and clear, to rouse
the day and say, Rejoice in her laughter!
—mornings when the sun commenced its decalogue
and scrawled a large and silent golden *aleph*
on their table's white enamel top.

                                        *
Old masters and young mistresses
                              —young Huxley's crack,
who recommended museums for cruising snatch.
Yes, something made them giddy, got them wild. . . . And he,
reconnoitering the galleries, wanted to understand.
Were these mere paintings? The place was like a zoo,
a menagerie of bright and breathing angels
sunning happily on walls . . . gods on holiday among us,
great naked pelts and swatches of four elements and darkness . . .
among whom you sauntered, swam, kicked up sand, flirted, got tanned,
got laid, drank pop . . . opulent and gorgeous, indifferent
to eyes that lit them, stares they inflamed . . . anyone
could gawk forever . . . at these overheating geniuses
in their stalled flotilla . . . unmindful of each other,
large jubilant babes in a marble playpen, each one
the president of everything . . . not civic types at all . . .
stars . . . but how accommodating, in grandeur and pleasure,
willing to shove over—and go on shining! . . .
their pantheon always with room for one more . . .
and why not? in this anthology of exile where they
no longer mattered . . .
                          What brought him to the bronze head
was the girl eye to eye, even nose to nose, with it
—to read its secret or to ask, as perhaps she asked

of everything, her own powers . . . whether to heal
or hurt . . . Of her he thought to recall the bright wad
of coppery hair and tan raincoat's diving hem,
its line exactly that a ship makes going down . . .
in this sumptuous flotsam of angel-animals . . .
He recognized the type: bright, abrupt, ungainly, confused,
patronizing the men she knew . . . other men made her nervous.
Well, which was he? wimp? or wolf? She never looked back.
The master must be losing his touch—though not his feeling
of connection with whatever woman he came across . . .
And was she dragging a leg? In fact? Or mockery?
And if mocking him, what sort of devil was he? Little, of course.
Oh where, he asked, have all the junior muses gone
who used to waltz within this sacred grove?

The bronze

was beautiful, a girl of eighteen,
he guessed, mouth and cheek still
delicate, her steady gaze
as if she held a moving thing
in view, flame or wave, himself.
What moved in him—broken or restless—
grew well, was still.

The stillness glowed.

Her hair, upswept in a budding wing,
poised for the lift of a lively word.
Like someone at the starting point
who asks both blessing and direction
she was waiting for him to speak.

*

A moving trance within a crowd,
she lagged its pace but, ferried on

the powerful forward surge, stopped
at the light with it, then crossed when
the crowd crossed Fifth Avenue. How many
days like this? in a thin dark slip,
barefoot, her blond hair knotted, hands
empty, her slim legs streaked with urine
and dirt, hardly able to lift her feet.
—Disaster must appear so when it looms
incontinent and purseless in the doorway,
with nothing in mind but barren motion.
And he, having rushed ahead and then
turned back again to help her, met
the perfect blankness of her gaze.
Dazed. Out to lunch. Nobody there.
More communion from an insect's glare.
He felt the world had lost its eyes,
himself vanishing in their empty noon.
She seemed as if beaten in broad daylight
and when no one intervened to save her,
she, too, couldn't stop to care, agreed
that she was nothing, superfluous, dust.
And drifted—panic's slowest immigrant
blown here out of the exploded future
to be the specter in the crowd's bad dream,
the person missing in the middle of the street,
beneath the mercy of anything.
Wake up, dear sister, he was trying to say
to the sibyl in her trance, but the woman
would not respond, so deep the charm that held her.
And the spell she was under was the end of the world.

FLIGHT FROM
THE CENTER

Geometry and concrete of the moonlit suburbs of the home-land dreaming under the eyes of high pilots.

At the antipodes of the globe underlying their parents' beds, guns at the ready, boys leap from trucks at dawn and sniff the thrill of havoc in smashed timbers, in burning thatch. It is like a tribal memory—they, too, want to move on out, and out. Suddenly, the huddling refugees stampede for the ditch. They gun their motors and lean back. The throbbing pulse eases toward a coffee break, the voices banter, bitch about the weather.

Unfathomable this peace the pilots patrol—a lone carlight, the homeward, belated traveler adrift in the shimmering grids! Hands frozen to the controls, they climb to the threshold of ice, out of touch, unable to divide enemy from friend, diving along the empty orbit . . .

JUST ANOTHER SMACK

Schoolmaster Auden gave them full marks,*
"the Old Masters," for having understood
"about suffering" its "human position."
The view from Mt. Lectern was clear. They were,
he noted, *"never wrong."*
                    One is pleased to see
things put in place, grateful for instruction
—though words like his might well inspire Job
with ruddied fingernails once more to rasp
excruciating music from festers and boils.
Sir, respectfully, is it possible
ever to be *right* about "suffering?"
—suffering which, after all, is not
just lying around waiting to be mapped,
but has abundantly its awful life.
I mean, sir, our suffering is no
Nativity, is never legendary
like Innocents slaughtered, Icarus plunging.
We lack that consolation. *Our* suffering
is nameless (like us) and newly whelped
and dying just to claim us for itself.

Perhaps, sir, you never meant all that,
had merely called in Birch the Learned

* *In his* "Musée des Beaux Arts."

to make the new-boy romantics smart:
Let them not think their feelings so damned
important, that sort of rubbish and rot!
And one does grant a classic wisdom here
that *could* help young masters get to be old.
I mean: When they pass out the suffering,
don't insist on getting yours—you make sure
you're the one "just walking dully along."
The other bloke's never hurts as much.

And let's suppose you've gotten off clean,
left that little problem to be brought up
by others, and yourself "sailed calmly on"
into Snug Harbor. Well, twenty years later,
and now your life's a lovely picture,
and you just settling down to enjoy it.
Looks pretty good from where you sit,
lots of bright colors smack in the center,
with some poor slob getting the shaft
off in a murky corner—*he* won't be missed.
Why, will it to a fine museum, that's
what you'll do!
                              And then wouldn't you know it.
Out cruising, say, for a little action,
or maybe looking to change its luck,
Suffering just happens to happen by,
big as leviathan and calling you son,
and clouts enormously your shoulder blade,
and dispatches a knee swift to the groin
—by now you haven't breath to shout
or to curse the day you were born—

and caves in your ear with a whisper
(the last words you're going to hear,
doubled over now, dropping fast),
"Listen close. It's me. Only *I* got away.
And my message is strictly for you
—Hey, old fella, you've been elected."

PROGRESS

para Frances y Manuel Velarde

1

History becomes prophecy becomes
history in time: lurching forward
on three wheels, the dialectic over-
rides the dialect, the lowly local
mud and straw; its spiraling logic mimes
and makes obsolete the seasons.
                                        So here
on this university building wall,
the universal on tour makes Mexico
its moral in Siqueiros's famous mural: see,
its symbolic sentimentalized citizens
—monumental mannikins, candle stumps
on the cake of a five-year plan—its pencil
like a club, its steel skeleton of girders,
its compasses, its banners on parade.
Siqueiros made it well: the brutal fore-
shortenings and blatant hyperkinesis
(dear to illustrators of action and sport)
successfully elbow the eyeball of
the beholder with Progress's big *kapow*,
the Forward march! of its roundhouse
haymaker Sunday knockout punch.

And facing it, across a hundred yards
or so of campus grass: a service strip

—bank, post office, bookstore—where buses stop,
in its midst a spot, not five yards square,
where an old tree, a tiny *colorín*, grows,
flowerless now although in full if not
extravagant leaf.

                Here you will see
an old straw hat hung on the stump
of a lower limb, and elsewhere among the branches
a worn jacket and bright straw basket
and two network sacks bulging with food;
against the tree, a long-handled tray
for gathering litter up; on the ground,
a cardboard box to put it in.
Here is a quiet shrine to work
and rest, their rhythm, delicate,
varying, certain as the leaves
turning in the wind or turning with
the seasons.

                Now, from behind the *colorín*,
a fat old man, the guardian, comes out,
sweeping with a straw broom all ten
dusty feet roundabout, and, grumbling, eyes
mistrustfully the stranger who,
camera at the ready, infringes here.
He doesn't know he's obsolete and charming,
he only finds *you* alarming, seems to think
the ground is his, not history's—you can see
he's just itching to take his broom to you
and send you flying with the dust.

2

Not the mural's clarion, great sonic
boom, benevolent rapist, big wind
turning the leaves all one way, more
monstrousness than any season will bear
—he is tactful and delicate,
to each one whispering a different thing,
what alone can win assent to justice,
to forgo the bitter privilege
of one's grievance against everything
—for who will be just to others
who has not been just to himself?—
possessing, in an instant, all
one's resentment claimed, giving it up,
turning as the *colorín* turns
shedding a thousand diffident gleams
now in its ordinary ecstasy.
Too slowly to be history, working
his way from heart to reluctant heart,
messiah has been here from the first,
busying himself about the tree.

IDEAL DISORDERS

Miles of rows of orange trash cans
all ah-ing to the sky was somebody's
idea of order at Coney Island;
another guy thought up the morning crew's
ragged line and lowered eyes—the daily stalk
of Parks Department foragers in green
straggling on heavy shoes and dreamily
lancing gum wrappers into gunny sacks.
Neither was anybody's idea of fun
—which was more like *dis*order, more like
just dropping public verticality
for open lolling about and wallowing,
down at sea level, off-guard, up-ended;
more like everybody getting together
and making a sea of "all of us"
alive beside the sea, ourselves
earth's numberless sands outfacing
the mirror shattered below the whole sky,
the slow monster under the empty motion.
Our being there was beelines over bodies,
was shortcuts swarming toward pleasure,
and half the fun was keeping it short,
and more than fun our thatch and hubbub,
our pullulation, of crossing purposes

filling the silence on the waters—until,
from the groin of comings and goings,
at three, at half past three exactly,
we hurled off a blanket to the day's height
the flying youth and cheering crowd—the sun!—
and peopled space with celebration.

A NEW WORLD

Torn maps, pages in spume
Crashing furniture of the shore
The nimble students leaping off,
who always from farther out
come riding toward us,
straddling desktops of the waves
—the water's glittering people,
the little pilgrims of light.

For these wavelets' chancing greenhorns,
our parents as they were, our future kids,
we the children of immigrants
walk in greeting at water's edge
and sing out the primer of fresh air:
Sky, president of thunder and smiles,
many-headed senates of the sea,
the jetties' bearded dripping courts,
and bully spanked home to his bad castle,
old death voted down the cellar stairs.
Everything, set free, arrives and shines.
All is a globe of recognitions.
Every creature of the place
—Utah, Kentucky, Idaho—
lit with intelligence,
glows as if about to speak;
wherever we look is looking back
with our gazes' own intensity,
the sun comes up, the waves
come up, asking our names.

And who *are* we, standing around
in bathing suits on the brink of everything?
We are Americans at the beach.

White confusions
Springs of the sea-winds' surging
—inland
toward mountains and prairies,
toward happiness.

THE GYMNASTS

Legs v-ed out from the groin's nugget
—the many figured as a single man.
Or the milling centipede of crossed purposes
pulling itself together and rising
from the ground up, in honor of itself.
And not to form the structures only, but
to be present in the flesh and confirmed
by others present equally to them
—leaving as early almost as the sun,
they come down from separate rooms, starting
from Elizabeth or Hoboken or the Bronx,
walking on their hands among us now
or spelling out with their spinning persons
leaping sentences of cartwheels and vaults.
Nearby, the body-builders are defining
their "pecs," biceps, "glutes"—glowing maps
of somber worlds in single display,
so distant that they sink slowly
into the background of every sky.
But here the gymnasts build themselves
together, embody what they illustrate:
serenity of power in action, strength
moving in matters of common concern;
and, by wall or mound or pyramid,
by honeycomb, womb, huddle, swarm
and tower—these sociable forms, forms
of habitation—in the middle of nowhere
bestow a sense to everything.

THE TOWER

A tower of men,
a tongue toward flaming heaven.
Now the last one goes up quick,
scaling fire to reach the baby
in the window of the burning tenement.
Everywhere, jealous angels look down.
The tower blazes up higher.
The faces puff in fury.
If we had breath to call him back . . .
His daring that makes the world come true.
—Arms uplifted,
he holds the whole sky open,
plucks the radiance from the fire,
the baby Now from the sky's *never!*
Oh, we gasp, Ah, we breathe out.

                                    Just
as quick, the tower tumbles apart,
leaping every which way down.
Their yawp sends them crashing off,
shin and thigh, to slaughter waves.
And we, set free, have walked away
on the sand's radiant reaches.

                                    Now
the little kids go racing after
and smack up geysers, shouting.

THE ALL-STARS

As when the fielders put down their gloves
and take up bats in their hands and pose
in a row on the dugout steps,
leaning forward, one foot on the field,
each in his own team's uniform,
each excelling at his specialty,
at the bunt or long ball or hit
and run or hitting where they ain't
or going with the pitch, each poised
within the flawless coincidence
of his competence and his name
—in token whereof his smile is grave,
leaving us to imagine the ball
stung on a line up the alley,
its mountain-making arc majestic
or tricky hop through a fielder crouching:

so it is we cave dwellers, rousing
to all that rumor in the stands,
stare from our own opposing dugout,
the heart's dark old colliery of awe,
and see—through the pure optic of fame—
daylight and then that pantheon
suddenly, like a burst of brilliants,
scatter across the great diamond
and take possession of the sunny air.

READ TO THE ANIMALS,
or ORPHEUS AT THE SPCA

A woman called and offered me a hundred dollars to read in San Francisco. I said, "Okay, but only for dogs and cats." "What?" she said. I said, "I charge five hundred dollars to read for people, but I'm interested in how pets respond to poetry. They hear humans speaking all the time, and I'm curious if they can tell the difference between ordinary speech and poetry." "Can't a few people be there too?" "No," I said, "five hundred dollars for people, one hundred dollars for household pets. I can only give so many readings a year, and I want to earn the most from them." So she said, "I don't see the difference. You're reading anyway, whether to dogs and cats or to people." She's dead serious about this. I said, "Well, the dogs and cats don't tell anyone how long you read or how much you gave it."

Philip Levine, interviewed in *Antaeus*, Summer 1980.

Dear Mr. Levine,
                        You can call me Rex.
I am a two-year-old male dog—big, short-haired,
mostly shepherd—living the last six months
in this here shelter for wayward animals.

  I read in a magazine how you looking
  —this what you told a poet lady friend
  of yours you called up on the telephone—
  to adopt a cat. Me too. Even if

I am canine, living with them day in
day out, I can say they totally cute.
Which probably is why they never seem
enough to go around. So flash on this:
our bitches really been getting the job done
—so maybe you adopt "some *puppy*" instead?

I also seen how you looking to read
your poetry to us. We all were jumping.
We don't have budget for poetry reading,
so all of us guys been saving up for you.
Cool you cutting your fee. I pretty sure
we be able to hack the hundred bucks.
Supervisor say she be writing to you
on official paper, she say anyhow
after you seen our facility, you want
to turn it all back to our building fund.
But I say, Tell her to go stuff, yeah! I say,
Keep it—cost of cat *always* going up!

Lot of poets starting to come around.
We animals got to be *in* thing now.
Bet you surprised how much poetry we dig.
Dickey, he read here couple a three times.
Ginsberg too. They charge humans thousands a pop,
but they wouldn't even take nothing from us.
I really dug Ginsberg's show—he got us
to sing along with him. *Om, om, om, om.*
Oh wow, us canines really turned on to that.

Hey, they both great kids. And both of them say
they will come to live here when they retire.

I can dig. How often they meet up with
a group that groove on their stuff—and show it?
Fame have got to be a mean trip: get yourself
disappointed, misunderstood—a touch too much
idolizing here, a touch too little there.
Got to be why big shots get down on mankind.
Then mankind turn around, give them the bum rap,
yeah, mankind say they stuck up on theirself.
I say they got to lick theirself front and back
—in the right doses, at the right times and places.
Hell, they never brag, if we gots art to praise them right!

Hey, bet you don't believe all the fans you got.
Every time *New Yorker* hit the catbox,
cats and dogs be fighting to read your poetry.
They really dig your deep humanity,
they dig your compassion for the underdogs.
They *know* you give them respect, feed them good,
never polish up your boot-tips on their bellies.
And be others here that get off on misery.
Pure breeds. Always be slumming. They kinky. They go,
"Oh, daddy, tell us what it like when you was poor!"
They *rub* their furs all *over* those fat pages.
Make me *sick* when they do that to your poetry.

Mr. Levine,
I was born in the streets.
Never knew my dad.
Never seen the inside of a house.
Never ate from a dish.
Never got to go on paper.

Yeah, I sniffed on the sidewalks,
I licked in the gutters
—I ain't shamed of that.
But now I want to make it to the top,
get to get 500 bucks a shot,
get to say anything I want to,
get to *go* on paper.
Get to beat the canine rap
—I be up there walking on two legs,
I be human, like god.

   Mr. Levine, you got to help me bad.
Hey, you adopt *me*, teach me to write poetry.
If they tell you no, then you sneak me out
after you read. Just wait till things quiet down,
then I tip you the high sign and we split.
But you watch out for Supervisor. Her bad.
Her Lady Cerberus. Her the Bitch Goddess.
Her never miss a trick. They's a whole bunch here
she caught already. Scottie and Papa,
Dylan, Delmore, Berries, Cal. She tell them,
You got to kiss my butt, 'cause this here the Hell of Fame.

   Mr. Levine, you lucky, you not famous,
but her *make* us famous, her make us household *pets*.
Give us fame-rabies just like them other cats.
I *seen* them on fire, raging and thrashing
to get theirself comfortable and couldn't
—their bodies all red with burning rashes,
like ten thousand hot tongues of wildfire rumor
was kissing them all over with their names,

telling them *who* they is. Pitiful how
they howl in pain, awful how they beg for more.
That fame, it's junk, and junk make you tame.
Best minds of my time foaming at the dentures!

   Got to cut out now. You remember what I wrote.
One way or other, I be busting this joint.
Hope this note don't smell too bad. Destroy it,
if you got to. Keep my secret.
                                        Rex.
                                  7/20/81

CONVERSATION ON A YAM

Fleas whose rag and beard I share,
whose body I inhabit barely
here on my backyard doxology
of four miserable yams
—Withered, Rotting, Frostbit, Green—
that I in a lifetime of effort
have dragged and huddled together;
today the easy fleas began
again, leaping up to see
this landscape of tumuli:
bare fields of bald personages,
each asquat his pile of yams
—inedible but good for building—
and about them gangs of hunched
and staggering smallish figures,
each of whom maneuvers in his arms
an offering larger than himself
toward one heap or other;
herniating with praise
and hardly acknowledged, he heaves
and hoists his pittance up
to the top of the daily tonnage.

Alighting, the leapers spoke to me.
The social commerce hereabouts
is heavy with homages.

Why this economy of praise?
"Because the delicate morale
of the high and the mighty
requires constant encomia
—else they get down in dumps,
too glum to banalize all others
to a vagueness of background, dim
screen for the flagrant cinema
of their own heroic figures.
Therefore each one clings to his hump."
But lively debates on culturing yams,
bracing acts of spiritual measurement,
wonderful questions of right and wrong
whose dextrous quibbling or quick evasion
keeps the suppliants supple . . .
                              "Are

beneath their masters' noses
delving the darkly measureless,
the mystery of themselves.
For this they need surpluses,
launchpads of panegyric
for hobnobbing with the stars,
hillocks of hymns and paeans
to reduce to a clear piddle
of personal essence."

The fleas leaped up—excellently
jet and joyous—and saw, and met
to meditate inside my rented ear.

. . . placatory gold hosannas they cram
under the high haunches of the great.

Because they like that moment at the top?
Hannibal's saddle also crossed the Alps
—and even the humblest porter at rest
will clamber onto his burden and sit.
The mighty, the mighty themselves thunder
to astound the little yammerer
gawking blindly in their dark insides.
"Let the great one's faith in himself
falter an instant, and the world
fails, too, his hand then palsies on
the hard levers, and the machinery
of affliction clatters on, masterless,
anonymous . . . "

                    How extraordinary
this awe you inflict on yourselves,
your craving for bosses and creation
of bullies, your hope to wreathe
the smeared harrow with the harrow's own
afflicted blooms!

                    "The hurtfulness
our mouths can name is the mordant
—and burns adoration into
the joyful animal throat,
inscribes a yam on the truthful tongue.
If there were no name to pray to, no name
to praise, how could we bear our pain?"

Bitter, bloodless, odorless, ocherous, cold
—among us the yam is not much esteemed.

Too bad. Remarkable creatures,
snoozing now in tune to my scratching,
I might have offered them a yam or two
for a song—sad short tally of praises
whose provenance I no longer recall
and that I ruminate and fuss,
boxing their compass too often,
into new and never less
unsatisfactory patterns.
Shall I climb off my yams?
Pull down my pile for good?
Take them out on the road?
Give them all away?
Unthinkable not to be in business.

But you, inching along in a furrow
under your burden, big or little, if
you hear my words and have a yam to give,
you know my name, you know where I live.

ELENA

Because she did such terrible things to them
with her sexiness and long, sauntering stride
and how she smiled and didn't avoid their eyes
but came right back with remarks of her own,
because day and night she wronged and injured them
with her height and olive skin and heavy jugs
—*Madonna mia!*—and the creeps she walked
around with but never walked with one of them,
because anyone could see her innocence,
that having no women's tricks, what she had
to defend herself from all the guys who came
poking and pushing at her was craziness,
yelling out dirty words to hurt their hearing
and dressing herself up crazy *and dumb*
—because of this the hard guys from Cherry Street,
they were the ones who busted into her flat
and pulled her boyfriend off her, worked him over,
broke his nose and chipped two teeth.

                                    And then because,
naked, bronze, tall, she stood there and never tried
to cover up while she yelled to let him go,
because of that they crapped all over the place,

they threw her underwear around and stomped it
—to tell her how she had confused and hurt them—
then, at wits' end, beat themselves off and scrammed,
having laid the tribute of their tantrum at
the altar of her high and white and double bed.

THE MEMORABLE

The poem on the page was always indeed
the same text, which is to say, the same stranger
encountered each time as if for the first time.
And like a stranger, it was greeted with questions:
Who are you? Where do you come from? What do you want?
—and was, finally, because it lacked a voice,
accosted with shamans and other diviners
who were voluble in answering for it.

The poem in the mind and in the mouth,
the remembered poem, spoke itself again.
It was a friend as close as one's own breath.
For the space of its speech, all other words
lay down in its voice and became its words.
Spoken by the poem, harkening as they spoke it,
even soothsayers and interpreters
grew idle and happy in a charm of feeling.

THE EPIPHANIES

Winter, the boardwalk,
the walkers moving into what,
neither visible nor unseen,
was clear sight, sheer immensity . . .
sun rinsing the stone fountains,
the bare herringbone old miles
of board . . . more mile and mile of sky
emptying toward Sandy Hook,
bright to pale, a whole openness
overhead, far out . . .
and the ocean composing gravely,
over and over, one verbiage,
fugitive, opulent, millions
of shadows, millions of lights
that rose and receded . . . rise and merge
in me as I write this out, now
as then are racing into being,
hold themselves out to shine
as I am stepping forward in the light.
Rare passersby who glance this way,
see, when we raise our arms and wave,
if light does not break on our lofty hands . . .
in one instant multitude walks the page,
in one gesture greeting and goodbye!
—we who nod and pass onward, each one
bearing brightness before him on his way.

HAPPINESS

It is very difficult not to be happy about blobs.

A blob appears to be a modestly elevated puddle, a failed puddle, so to speak.

Unlike a tragic hero, no quantity of negated life, no yearning, discipline, suffering, sacrifice, can make a blob a larger or more authentic blob.

By the same token, one can't save up to make a blob.

The first time in my life I rose on two legs, I looked down on the space vacated by my blob and I laughed.

One knows all of a blob in knowing any bit of it, but the whole blob gives more pleasure.

Together with its contentment and unfuzzy outline, this makes a blob an excellent household thing.

Heaven by any other name would be boring. A blob neither knows nor wishes to know another name for heaven.

There are not two kinds of blob, or two ways to be a blob.

Nor is it possible to distinguish between real and ideal blobs.

If I say, "A blob," I do not thereby banish every present blob. Nor do I bring any absent blob to mind.

A blob is like a happy ending—it leaves you free to walk away.

I have walked away from many blobs, but no blob has ever walked away from me.

Decidedly, it is difficult not to be happy about blobs.

THE GRAND MAGIC
THEATER FINALE

The curse was to claw the earth with their hands
in the dark until every cue was handed up.

And then the liberation of light blazing.
And here, out of their roles, the cast comes back
in costume—how shy they seem of those rich
stigmata—marking time, shambling their steps.
See, the stars, too, have lined up with the chorus,
turning to meet our eyes and gaze frankly
at last, face to face. And look at the lot
bust loose, stomp and prance, shake that dynamite.
There's nothing they don't over-over-over-do.
And what life they must have to be so different
every time we look! Like half-molted metaphors
—at ease in two worlds at once—they ad-lib
and swank their old impersonations for us
as if to say, *All that was just kidding.*
This happiness is the serious stuff.

Their exuberance, their soaring
would break our hearts if they weren't making
everything larger, ourselves immortal,
with laughter. And surely they must know it,
singing out louder, reaching out their arms to us.
And who can say what they are begging and bringing?

Our cheering says, *Freedom! Feeling!*—from which
they wave, riding high, blowing both-handed kisses,
What wonderful people—you're all angels.
Not goodbye but hello, folks, welcome to heaven!

TALKING TO FERNANDO

to my son

Life is swell like this, life is great,*
with everything going past all the time.
It's easy here—inside the speed,
just us sitting snug in the groove,
just us cruising on ahead.
Nothing's too fast, nothing too slow.
Hell, look, we've got no worries,
not when we're rolling like this.
We don't need anything else.
Things are smooth, right? things are fine,
nothing could be better than this.
Take the wheel whenever you like.
And when I drive, you don't have to talk,
you can sleep, you can look out the window
—that's cool, that's okay, everything's okay
as long as we keep on going this way.

I'll tell you what.
I want to give you something.
I want to give you a lot.
If I've got it, you can have it.
Want my Harley chopper? It's yours.
I'll throw in the windjammer fairing.

After Jean Giono.

I'll throw in the slipstreamer 'shield.
I'll give you the stereo deck.
Really, I want you to have it.
Just name it, you've got it.

Meanwhile, it's so great this way.
Even when we get to New York
we don't have to stop—I mean it.
We can keep on going.
We can go all night like this,
we can go all year.
What the hell, we can go anywhere.
How does California sound?
I bet you we could make Peru.

Listen, I'll give you my golden helmet,
the one with the little decals you liked.
You see? I didn't forget.
I'll give you the silver jacket
I won shooting craps last year.
Remember my new green boots,
the ones with the fancy tooling?
I'll give you them, too.
I'll give you my honey gloves.

Irving Feldman was born in Coney Island, New York, in 1928 and attended City College and Columbia University. He has taught at the University of Puerto Rico, Kenyon College (Ohio), and the University of Lyon, in France. His poems have appeared in *The New Yorker*, *Harper's*, *The Atlantic*, *Partisan Review*, and many other magazines; two of his previous collections, *The Pripet Marshes* and *Leaping Clear*, were nominated for the National Book Award, in 1966 and 1977. Mr. Feldman is professor of English at the State University of New York at Buffalo. This is his seventh book of poems.